Your Body and Health

CELLS
AND REPRODUCTION

Jen Green

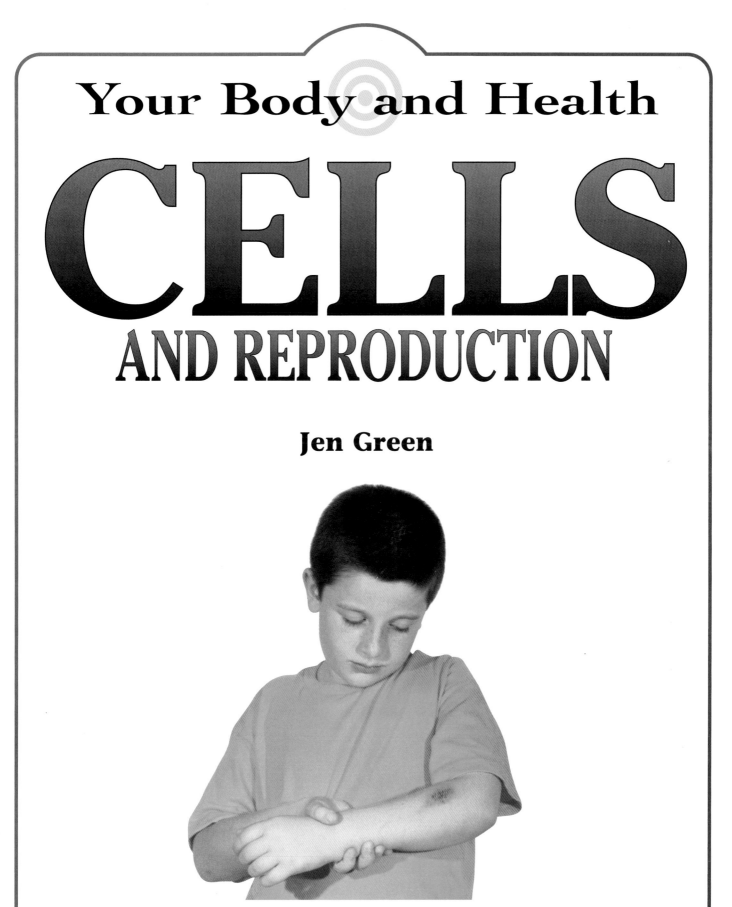

STARGAZER BOOKS

© Aladdin Books Ltd 2006

Produced by Aladdin Books Ltd

First published in the
United States in 2006 by:
Stargazer Books
c/o The Creative Company
123 South Broad Street
P.O. Box 227
Mankato, Minnesota 56002

Editor: Katie Harker

Designer:
Flick, Book Design & Graphics
Simon Morse

Illustrators:
Aziz A. Khan, Simon Morse,
Rob Shone, Ian Thompson

Certain illustrations have appeared in earlier
books created by Aladdin Books.

Printed in Malaysia

Medical editor: Dr. Hilary Pinnock

Dr. Pinnock is a GP working in Whitstable, UK. She
has written and consulted on a variety of medical
publications for all ages.

Library of Congress Cataloging-in-Publication Data

Green, Jen.
    Cells and reproduction / by Jen Green.
        p. cm. -- (Your body and health)
    Includes index.
    ISBN 1-59604-052-1
    1. Reproduction--Juvenile literature. 2.
    Embryology--Juvenile literature. 3. Cytology--
    Juvenile literature. I. Title.

QP251.5.G744 2005
612.6--dc22
                            2004058614

Contents

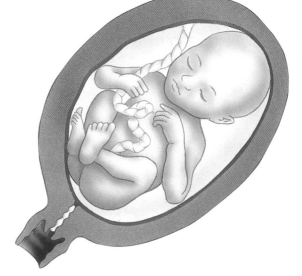

Introduction

All living things, from towering trees to tiny animals, are made of units called cells. The simplest life-forms are made up of just one cell, while larger living things contain billions of cells. All living things reproduce so that their species does not die out. Reproduction is the amazing process that results in all living things, including you! This book tells you all you need to know about your cells and reproductive system and how to keep them in good condition for a healthy body.

Medical topics

Use the red boxes to find out about different medical conditions and the effects that they can have on the human body.

You and your cells

Use the green boxes to find out how you can help improve your general health and keep your cells and reproductive system in good condition.

The yellow section

Find out how the insides of your body work by following the illustrations on yellow backgrounds.

Health facts and health tips

Look for the yellow boxes to find out more about the different parts of your body and how they work. These boxes also give you tips on how to keep yourself really healthy.

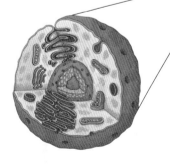

What is reproduction?

Reproduction is the process by which living things produce young, so that their kind continues. Living things reproduce in two main ways. Simple life-forms such as marine organisms (below) split to form two identical creatures. In most animals, including humans, a male and female mate to produce new offspring. This is called sexual reproduction.

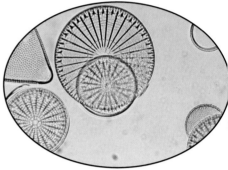

Reproduction results in new life. Human parents produce children who eventually grow into adults that can have children of their own.

Systems of the body

In the human body, cells do not work on their own, but in groups of similar cells. Groups of one cell type grow to form tissues such as bone and muscle tissue. Groups of different tissues form organs—such as the heart or kidneys. Organs then work together to form body systems such as the digestive and circulatory system.

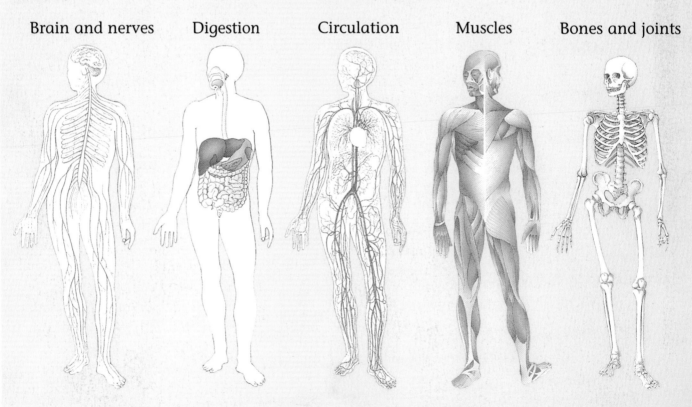

Brain and nerves   Digestion   Circulation   Muscles   Bones and joints

Reproductive organs

The reproductive organs are the body parts involved in producing young. The male reproductive parts include glands named testes (testicles) that produce male sex cells called sperm. These leave the body via the penis. The female reproductive parts include glands named ovaries, that produce female sex cells named eggs or ova. These pass into the uterus (womb). If an egg is fertilized by a sperm, a baby develops and grows in the womb.

Cells

Most of the cells in your body are tiny—only one-thirtieth of a millimeter across on average. They can only be seen using a microscope. There are over 200 types of cells in the human body, including red blood cells (left). Body cells vary greatly in size, shape, and function.

The male reproductive organs

The female reproductive organs

Changing cells and new life

Cells are the smallest units capable of independent life. All living things, however big or small, carry out certain processes that keep them alive. They need oxygen and nutrients to survive. Living things also move and grow, produce waste, and can sense and respond to their surroundings. All living things eventually die, but may reproduce to replace themselves. The cells of living things carry out all of these vital processes.

Some cells, such as those in your digestive system, live for just a few days. Skin and blood cells live for a few weeks, while some nerve cells last a lifetime.

Mitosis 1
When ordinary cells divide, the nucleus splits to form two "daughter" cells that are identical.

Growth and new cells

For living things to grow, new cells must be made. Growth happens as cells divide. Ordinary body cells divide by a process called "mitosis" to produce two identical cells. Sex cells multiply through a different process, called "meiosis," which produces two cells that are not identical.

Mitosis 2
Each cell has a set of instructions called genes (see pages 10-11), to carry out its work and make new cells.

New life
Babies begin life as a single fertilized cell, produced when an egg from the mother joins with a sperm from the father.

Meiosis

Meiosis and sexual reproduction produce unique forms of new life (left). Eggs and sperm cells are produced by the process of meiosis. The nucleus of the sex cell divides to form two cells. These new cells are not identical, and only contain a half-set of instructions. The other half is provided when the egg and sperm join, in a process called fertilization (see pages 12-13).

Growth and repair

Cells all over your body divide through mitosis as you grow and develop from a baby into a child and then an adult. Even when you are grown up, your cells continue to divide to heal injuries, replace worn-out cells, and keep parts such as nails and hair growing.

Mental growth

As you grow up, you absorb a huge amount of information about the world around you. All this learning takes place in the brain, as new connections are established between tiny nerve cells. Changing cells in your brain also help you to develop emotionally. Humans take longer to grow up than other animals—probably because we have a lot to learn!

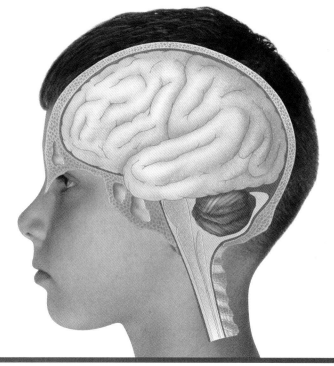

The body's building blocks

You have around 50 trillion (million million) cells in your body. Some tiny living things, like bacteria, are made up of just one cell.

Cells are like miniature laboratories where the chemistry of life takes place. Like tiny factories, cells are always busy doing vital work for the body. Cells throughout your body make vital chemicals and divide to form new cells. They take in food, use oxygen to break it down to release energy, and create waste. Different cells carry out different jobs around the body.

Structure of a cell

Most cells contain a nucleus, which tells the cell how to function. A jellylike material called cytoplasm surrounds the nucleus. Cells also contain structures called organelles, which carry out particular jobs and work like mini-organs. These include mitochondria, which break down food to provide energy, and ribosomes, which make proteins. An outer skin or membrane encloses the cell.

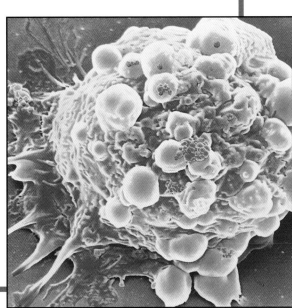

Membrane

Nucleus

Cytoplasm

Mitochondria supply energy.

Ribosomes make proteins for the cell.

Cancer

Cancer is a general name for a group of illnesses in which cells become unhealthy and start to multiply out of control. When this happens the cells no longer work properly, and may form a lump, or "tumor" (right). We don't know exactly why cells become cancerous, but genes, diet, and the environment all play a part.

Cell types

Cells are the body's "building blocks," like the millions of tiny grains of sand that make up a sandcastle. Each has a particular shape that helps it carry out its work. Some of the main types of cells in your body are shown here.

Brain cells
Nerve cells such as brain cells are made of long, thin fibers. Nerve cells relay messages between the brain and the rest of the body.

Heart cells
Heart cells form a special type of muscle tissue named cardiac muscle. As the cardiac muscles tighten, the heart pumps blood around the body.

Lung cells
The cells that line your lungs allow oxygen to pass through into your bloodstream, and carbon dioxide to pass from blood into the lungs, to be breathed out.

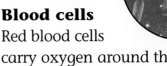

Blood cells
Red blood cells carry oxygen around the body. They have a flattened shape like doughnuts because this gives a larger surface area to carry oxygen.

Liver cells
Liver cells perform a variety of vital jobs for the body. For example, they store nutrients from your food and destroy poisons.

Muscle cells
Muscle cells are made of long, thin fibers that can shorten. Together they form muscles that tighten to pull on bones.

Bone cells
Bone cells build the skeleton that forms your body's framework. These cells produce the materials from which bones are made.

The secret of life

Have you ever been told that you look like your mom or dad? This is because the fertilized cell from which you grew contained instructions, called genes, from your parents. This mix of genes created a blueprint for a whole new person—you. Genes are written in code on little x-shaped structures named chromosomes, found in the nucleus of cells. They control features such as your height and hair color.

The fine threads of DNA inside chromosomes are amazingly long. If enlarged to the size of a hose, a DNA molecule would stretch 6 miles (10 km)!

Chromosome

Cell

Chromosomes
The nucleus in every cell in your body contains slender, x-shaped structures named chromosomes. These are made up of tightly coiled molecules of DNA.

Genes

Genes are sections of DNA (deoxyribonucleic acid) that contain instructions for a particular feature, such as the color of your eyes. Each tiny x-shaped chromosome carries thousands of these little snippets of information.

DNA
Molecules of DNA have a special structure, like a twisted ladder. The ladder's rungs are made of four chemicals that pair up to form long sequences, which are genes.

Cells through the body contain 23 pairs of chromosomes. You get one set of chromosomes from your mother and one from your father.

Grandparents   Grandparents

Father   Mother

You!

Inheritance

Children resemble their parents because they inherit features from them, through their genes. When the sperm containing your dad's genes joined with the egg with your mom's genes, the genes mixed together to create a unique blend, which resulted in you. Your parents inherited features from *their* parents—your grandparents. Do you resemble your dad's or mom's side of the family most?

Genetic cure

Inherited illnesses such as cystic fibrosis (a lung disease) and thalassemia (a blood disease) are caused by faulty genes, which pass down from parents to their children. Scientists are working hard to identify the different genes that make us more susceptible to diseases.

In future, the use of genetic engineering could help repair faulty genes and prevent particular diseases from developing.

Genetic engineering

In a new technique known as genetic engineering, scientists can combine the characteristics of two different species by taking sections of DNA and inserting them into the DNA of another developing species. Scientists can also create exact copies or clones of animals using a related technique. Instead of having genes from a mother and a father, a clone has genes from just one parent.

Your code

The order in which the four chemicals of DNA appear forms a set of instructions—just as letters of the alphabet combine to form words and sentences.

The reproductive process

As you grow up, your body starts to change to make it possible for you to have children of your own one day. Every human child begins when a man and a woman have sex or "make love," and a sperm from the man fuses with an egg inside the woman's body. If the egg is successfully fertilized, a baby will start to grow inside the woman's womb until it is ready to be born.

Female sex cells, or ova, are among the largest cells in the body, measuring nearly 0.004 inches (0.1 mm) across. Sperm cells are tiny in comparison.

Reproductive organs

In humans, the reproductive organs are found in or near the lower abdomen. In males, the testes are contained in a skin bag named the scrotum, which hangs between the legs. The reproductive parts start to function after puberty (see pages 22-23).

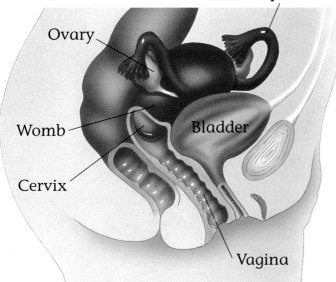

Fallopian tube
Ovary
Womb
Bladder
Cervix
Vagina

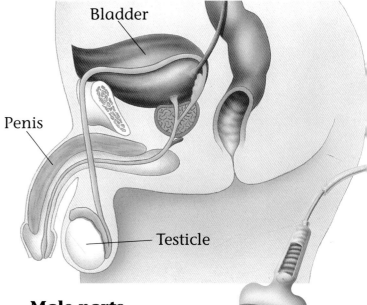

Bladder
Penis
Testicle
Sperm

Female parts
A woman's ovaries produce eggs. When ripe (see page 13), they pass down the fallopian tubes which lead to the uterus (womb).

A fertilized egg develops in the womb. Unfertilized eggs pass through the narrow neck of the womb (the cervix), to leave the body via the vagina.

Egg

Male parts
A man's testes produce millions of tiny, tadpole-shaped sperm every day. These swim by thrashing their long tails. Sperm may be stored in a coiled tube named the epididymis for several days, or may leave via the penis in a milky fluid called semen.

Egg production

Each of the woman's ovaries contains hundreds of unripe egg cells. These ripen under the control of body chemicals named sex hormones. Each month, one egg ripens and pops out of its protective case to travel down the fallopian tube. The empty case later helps to produce more sex hormones.

Developing egg

Ovary

Released egg

Empty case

Blood vessels

Sperm race

About 300 million sperm are released, but only a hundred or so swim as far as the fallopian tubes to reach a ripe egg.

As the sperm cluster around the egg, each tries to penetrate the outer membrane to fuse with the egg.

If the nucleus of one sperm enters the egg, the membrane changes to prevent other sperm from entering.

Egg

Ovary

Sperm

Womb

Conception

Conception, or fertilization, is the vital moment when new life begins. When a man and woman have sex, the man's penis gets larger and stiffens, so it can be placed into the woman's vagina. At the climax of love-making, the penis releases millions of sperm that swim up through the womb, toward the fallopian tubes.

Pregnancy

A pregnant woman often feels hungrier than usual, as she is "eating for two"—both herself and the baby.

After mating, most female animals lay tough-shelled eggs, in which the young develop outside the mother's body. Puppies, kittens, and other baby mammals develop differently. They grow inside the mother's body during pregnancy. When the babies are fully developed, the mother gives birth. Humans develop in the same way, spending nine months in the womb before birth.

Fertilized egg

Growth begins

After a few hours, the fertilized egg cell splits into two cells, then four, eight, and so on. By the fifth day it has become a ball of about a hundred cells, called a blastocyst.

Problems in pregnancy

If a fertilized egg develops in the fallopian tube, causing pain and bleeding (an "ectopic pregnancy"), the cells will need to be removed by surgery. If an egg develops low in the womb, the placenta may block the cervix (a "placenta previa"). In this case, a Caesarian section may be needed.

Blastocyst

Boy or girl?
The gender (sex) of the growing baby is determined by two types of chromosomes, called X and Y chromosomes. The fertilized egg receives one from each parent. The mother's is always X, but the father's may be X or Y. If the resulting mix is an XX, the baby will be a girl. An XY combination produces a boy.

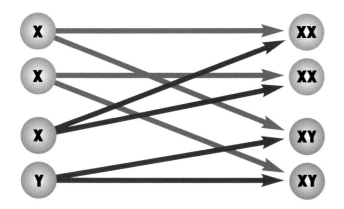

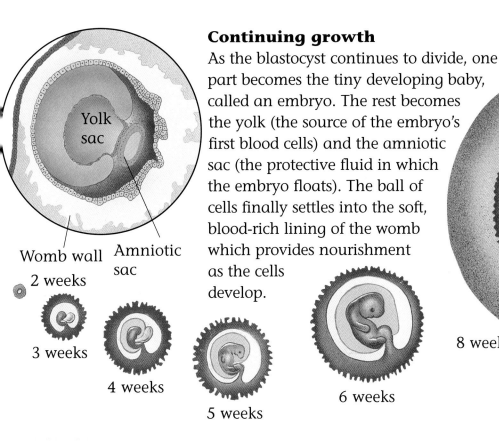

Yolk sac

Womb wall

Amniotic sac

2 weeks

3 weeks

4 weeks

5 weeks

6 weeks

8 weeks

Actual size

Continuing growth

As the blastocyst continues to divide, one part becomes the tiny developing baby, called an embryo. The rest becomes the yolk (the source of the embryo's first blood cells) and the amniotic sac (the protective fluid in which the embryo floats). The ball of cells finally settles into the soft, blood-rich lining of the womb which provides nourishment as the cells develop.

The developing embryo

As the embryo's cells continue to divide, so they start to specialize, becoming brain, bone, and blood cells, and all the other types of body cells. By the age of three weeks, the brain and backbone have formed. At four weeks, the heart begins to beat. By eight weeks, the tiny shape is starting to look more human, with a face, chest, abdomen, arms, and legs. The unborn child is now called a fetus.

Twins

Do you have twins in your family? Non-identical twins develop if two eggs from the ovaries are fertilized by two sperm at the same time. Identical twins result if the fertilized egg splits and develops into two separate embryos. Triplets, quadruplets, and other multiple births form in a similar way.

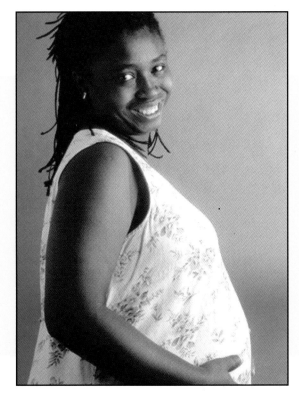

Changing shape

The mother's belly gradually swells to fit the baby growing inside her. By around 16 weeks, the fetus is about 5 in [11 cm] long, and now starts to grow quickly. By about 20 weeks the mother can feel her baby kicking. The fetus reaches about half its birth weight by about 28 weeks, and full size by 38 weeks.

Preparing for birth

Baby birds and reptiles hatch from tough-shelled eggs. Most mammals are born in a different way—from the womb of their mother.

After about 12 weeks in the womb, unborn babies become more active. They spend most of their time sleeping, but may also stretch and kick to flex their muscles. At about 38 weeks, the baby is ready to be born. The first sign is often when the "water breaks," as the amniotic sac bursts, and the liquid flows out. Now the muscles of the womb begin to squeeze, to push the baby out.

Ultrasound

A technique named ultrasound allows doctors to "see" a baby's development inside the womb. High-pitched sound waves travel through the mother's skin to bounce back off the fetus. These echoes are then displayed as an image on the screen.

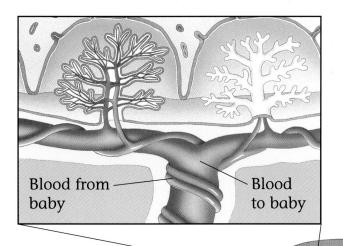

Blood from baby

Blood to baby

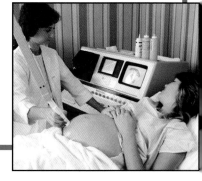

Getting nourishment
The baby's blood passes down its umbilical cord, into long "fingers" of tissue named villi in the placenta. There the baby's blood flows alongside its mother's. Oxygen and nourishment pass from the mother's blood into the baby's blood, in exchange for carbon dioxide gas and other waste.

Amniotic fluid

Umbilical cord

The placenta

Unborn babies get the oxygen and nourishment they need from their mother, via a blood-rich organ called the placenta. This is attached to the womb and to a long tube called the umbilical cord, linking the child to the mother. This cord is cut after the baby is born and later drops off, leaving a bellybutton.

16

1 Birth begins

As the time for birth approaches, most babies turn upside-down, so the head will emerge first. Being born feet-first is called a "breech birth."

Gestation times

Gestation is the time between conception and birth. Most mammals have a shorter gestation time than humans. Puppies spend two months in the womb, mice just three weeks. However, whales and elephants have a longer gestation than humans: 10-15 months for whales, and 22 months for elephants.

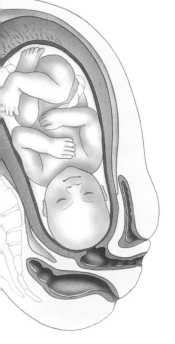

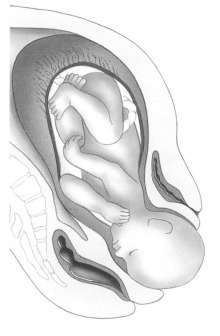

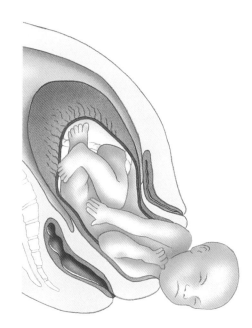

Giving birth

What do you know about your birth? How long did it take? Were you born head-first, as most babies are, or feet-first? When you were ready to be born, your mother "went into labor." Her womb started to contract (tighten), gently at first, then more strongly, to squeeze you out. After hours of hard work, you finally emerged into a big new world.

2 Labor continues

As the womb continues to contract, the cervix (narrow neck of the womb) widens. The baby's head turns sideways to pass through this opening more easily.

3 Out at last

The baby's head appears and is soon followed by the rest of the body. Most babies then start to cry, which opens the airways and lungs.

Birth problems

Problems sometimes develop during birth. If the birth is too slow, doctors may use forceps to gently ease the baby out. Sometimes, a cut is made in the mother's abdomen to deliver the baby by "Caesarian section."

Infancy

Most babies cry to attract their parents' attention whenever they feel uncomfortable, for example if they are hungry, wet, tired, or too cold or hot.

Birth was the biggest single change that has ever happened to you! From the warm, dark womb, you arrived in a strange, bright world full of unfamiliar sights, sounds, and smells. With your keen sense of smell, you soon learned to recognize your mother's scent as she fed you. Loud sounds made you cry. At first you could only see objects at close range, and you soon learned to recognize the faces of your parents.

In need of help

Many young animals can stand and take care of themselves just hours after birth. But for many months, human babies rely heavily on their carers. Gradually, as a baby develops skills of coordination and gains in strength, it learns to support its own head and roll over. Most babies can sit, with help, by the age of five or six months.

Sleep patterns

Some babies sleep more than others. Some sleep only for brief snatches, others for hours on end. Gradually, parents introduce the idea that night is for sleeping! For parents this time can be exhausting, until the baby learns to sleep through the night.

Potty training

Babies and young children have no control over their bowels or bladder. Soft, absorbent diapers mop up the spills. When the time is right, parents begin potty training. Most children are able to stay dry, at least during the day, by about the time they begin school.

18

Baby food

Birds bring food for their young, but most young animals, including reptiles (above) have to find food for themselves. Mammals are unique in providing nourishing milk from their own bodies. Later, all baby mammals are weaned (their milk intake is reduced) and they begin to eat solid food.

Vaccinations

A vaccination is a weakened form of a disease that is usually given by injection, to guard against dangerous diseases. Most children are given vaccinations at an early age. Their immune system reacts by producing substances called antibodies to fight off the illness. If they later catch the disease, their body finds it easier to defeat.

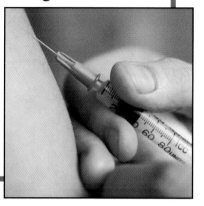

Milestones in development

Like most children, you were probably able to sit up by yourself by about eight months. A month or so later, you could crawl. By a year, you may have taken your first wobbly steps, and by about 14 months you were toddling. Children pass these "milestones" at slightly different times, but always in the same order.

Sitting up

Crawling

Walking

19

Growing and learning

Like all children, you grew fastest in the nine months before you were born, and during your first two years. Your growth then continued steadily as cells through your body multiplied. Growth is affected by many factors, including your genes and the food you eat. It is regulated by the pituitary gland in the brain, which produces growth hormone. As you grew bigger, you also learned a huge range of physical, mental, and social skills.

Babies learn to talk by copying the noises they hear around them. Gradually, gurgles and babbling sounds become recognizable words!

Talking, reading, and writing

By about one year old, most young children can say a few words. They then learn to link words to form simple phrases, and later complicated sentences. Reading and writing come later, often with the help of teachers at school.

Growing proportions

Parts of your body grow at different rates. A baby's head is large compared to other body parts, to hold its brain. By six years, the torso has caught up a bit, but limbs are still short. Then the limbs lengthen more quickly. An adult's head is fairly small in relation to the torso and limbs.

Head

Torso

Legs

2 years

6 years

9 years

11 years

Food for growth

A varied diet, including plenty of fresh fruit and vegetables, protein in the form of meat, fish, eggs, or beans, and carbohydrates such as bread or pasta, is vital for growing bodies. In poorer parts of the world, children who don't get enough to eat, or enough variety in their diet, don't grow as well and may not reach full size.

Coordination

As you grew physically bigger and stronger, you also learned to coordinate your movements. After walking and running became easy, you learned to hop, jump, ride a bike, and perform delicate tasks. Playing sports helps to fine-tune your coordination.

Growth problems

Some growth problems are caused by a poor diet, such as iodine deficiency (below). Others are caused by an imbalance of hormones in the body. If the pituitary gland produces too little growth hormone, children grow too slowly. If too much is produced, they grow too quickly. Doctors can correct some growth problems using medical drugs.

Social skills

As well as classroom learning and physical skills, you also learned vital social skills as you got older. By interacting with others, you learned to consider other people, share possessions, to plan and make decisions, and most of all, to make friends. These social skills become evermore important as you get older.

21

Approaching adulthood

Both boys and girls experience a growth spurt around puberty. Boys may grow as much as 3 inches (7.5cm) a year at this time.

As you enter your teens, physical changes take place in your body to make it possible for you to produce children. Some of these changes happen suddenly (like when a boy's voice "breaks"), while others develop more slowly. This time of physical change is called puberty. It is part of a greater change, called adolescence, as you grow up mentally as well as physically, to prepare for adulthood.

Puberty in girls

Around the age of 11, a girl's breasts begin to develop and her hips become more rounded. Hair grows around the genitals and under the armpits. The ovaries begin to produce ripe eggs and she begins to menstruate ("have periods"), as blood flows from the vagina for 2-7 days each month.

Periods

After puberty, the lining of a girl's womb thickens once a month, but breaks down and passes from the vagina if an egg is not fertilized. Taking care with hygiene and using tampons or pads (right) to absorb the bleeding, will keep your body fresh and healthy at this time.

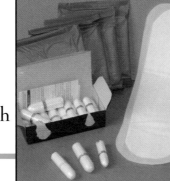

Puberty in boys

Puberty happens a little later in boys, usually at around 12 or 13 years. The boy's body becomes more muscular and later his voice "breaks," or deepens. Hair grows around the genitals and also in other places, including the face and chest. The testes begin to produce sperm and the male hormone testosterone.

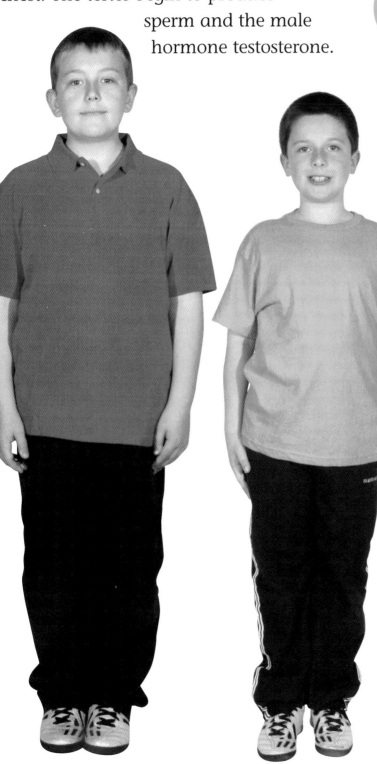

Acne
At puberty, the skin becomes more oily as your body chemistry changes. If oil or dead skin cells block the tiny openings in the skin from which hairs grow, acne (pimples) can develop.

Peer pressure
Adolescence is a time of change and trying new things. Your peers, or older people, may try to persuade you to do things like taking up smoking, trying illegal drugs, or having sex. However, having sex is a huge decision, and smoking and drugs are dangerous. You need to make up your own mind about these important issues, and not be swayed by others.

Dealing with emotions
Adolescence is a time of great emotional upheaval, as you adjust to the physical changes in your body, and also grow up mentally and emotionally. Your attitudes may change as you make new friendships, become sexually attracted to others, and perhaps start relationships. All this can seem overwhelming, but try to relax and it'll be easier to take things in your stride.

Planning a family

Animals such as sheep have now been cloned using techniques similar to IVF (see below right). However, cloning humans is against the law.

After puberty, you are physically able to have children. However, it will be some years before you gain the skills and experience needed to think about raising a family of your own. Of course, you need to meet the right partner, too. Many couples use contraception because they don't want to start a family immediately. Other couples find it difficult to have children. Infertility has various causes. Nowadays, infertility can often be helped by medical treatment.

The woman's cycle

Conception can only take place at a particular time during a woman's menstruation cycle. This "fertile period" occurs around ovulation, when the ripe egg is released from the ovary. The lining of the womb builds up at this time but breaks down if the egg is not fertilized.

Egg released around day 14

Womb lining thickest between days 20-25

Lining begins to break down around day 26

Menstruation cycle

| Cycle starts | 7 days | 14 days | 21 days | 28 days | Cycle begins again |

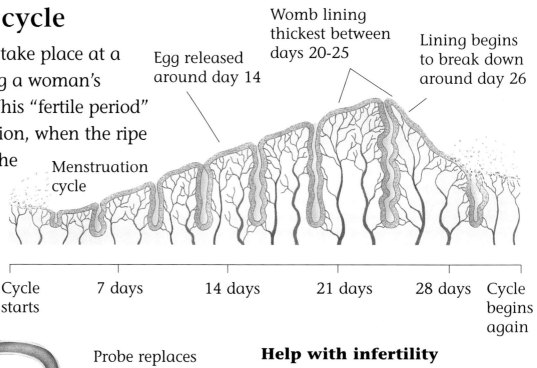

Probe removes ripe eggs from ovary

Probe replaces fertilized eggs in womb lining

Help with infertility
Some kinds of infertility can be helped by a technique called IVF (in vitro fertilization), in which eggs are fertilized outside the woman's body. The surgeon removes ripe eggs from the woman's ovaries using a probe (left), and then adds her partner's sperm to fertilize them. The fertilized eggs are then returned to the womb so they can develop in the normal way.

Smoking, drinking, & drugs

Smoking, drugs, and alcohol can all reduce fertility in both men and women. The effects of alcohol can lower a man's sperm count and impair the function of female sex hormones. Research has shown that binge drinking causes the most damage. Smoking, drugs, and alcohol can can also harm the health of unborn babies in the womb. That is why women are advised to avoid drinking, illegal drugs, and cigarettes when they are pregnant.

STDs

Sexually transmitted diseases (STDs) are infections that can be caught during sexual contact. They include chlamydia, venereal disease, genital warts, and also HIV, which leads to AIDS, an illness that attacks the body's immune system. Although STDs can affect anyone, using contraceptives and limiting the number of sexual partners that you have, reduces the risk.

Contraception

Contraception is used to avoid pregnancy. There are several methods available. Women can take a daily contraceptive pill. An IUD, or coil, may be fitted into a woman's womb. Barrier methods include a diaphragm worn over a woman's cervix, or a condom worn over a man's penis. Condoms are also used to prevent STDs.

Population explosion

There are now over six billion people in the world. In the last 50 years or so, the human population has grown dramatically. The increase is most rapid in developing countries, where large families are common and contraceptives are less widely used.

There has also been a marked increase in the number of teenage pregnancies. Practicing safe sex is important for your sexual health and also reduces the chances of you, or your partner, becoming pregnant.

Growing older

Every one of us is aging all the time. For example, you are just a little bit older now, than when you started reading this book! People reach their peak of strength and fitness around the age of 20. After that, we all begin to age, but the changes this causes happen so gradually that they are hardly noticeable for many years.

Frenchwoman Jeanne Calment currently holds the record for the oldest person. She lived 122 years (1875-1997).

Cells and aging

The main period of growth is between conception and about 20 years, when a person is fully grown. In later life, cell activity slows down and body parts work less well. However, improved levels of diet and fitness mean that most people can stay healthy for longer. Today, many active grandparents (right) enjoy their extended family!

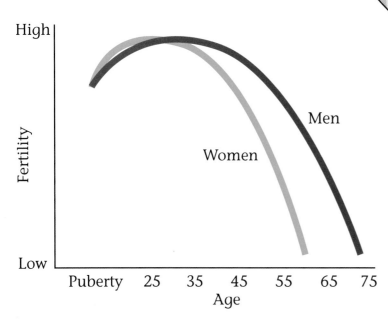

Fertility through the years

Girls become fertile around the age of 11 or 12, boys a few years later, about 13 or 14. Some time around the age of 50, the woman's menopause occurs (see page 27) and she can no longer have children. Men stay fertile for much longer, until the age of 70 or more.

The menopause

In later life, a woman's ovaries stop producing ripe eggs, and she stops having periods. This is called the menopause. It may happen as early as 45 or as late as 55. At the same time, the woman's body stops making the female hormone estrogen. This can cause uncomfortable hot sweats and mood swings. Some women start taking estrogen pills at this time—also known as Hormone Replacement Therapy (HRT).

Life expectancy

Life expectancy—how long you live—is affected by many factors, including your genes, diet, and the kind of life you lead. In developed countries where diet and health care are good, most people now live well into their 70s. In developing countries where diet and health are poorer, people generally don't live as long, mostly into their 50s.

Effects of aging

In later life, a variety of health problems may develop as cell replacement decreases. Some older people's bones become brittle so that they break easily, a condition called osteoporosis. Others suffer from rheumatism, as their joints swell or the cartilage that lubricates joints gets worn. Medical treatment can help to ease some of these problems.

Skin and aging

In later life skin loses its natural elasticity, and wrinkles develop. This is partly caused by exposure to the sun. People from sunny countries tend to have more wrinkles than people from cooler places. Always use sunscreen lotion to protect your skin from the effects of the sun.

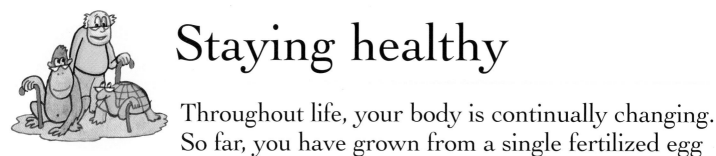

Staying healthy

Humans live longer than most other animals. Most small animals live only a year or two, but gorillas may live to 50, and tortoises to over 100.

Throughout life, your body is continually changing. So far, you have grown from a single fertilized egg cell into a large, complex animal made of millions of cells. You carry on growing until you reach the age of about 20. No one is sure why we stop growing. It may be that the body somehow counts the number of times that cells divide, and stops at a certain number. Taking good care of your body when you are young will help you enjoy a healthy old age.

Exercise

Exercise is vital to develop strong bones and muscles, and supple joints. Exercise also guards against health problems such as heart disease, because it prevents you from becoming overweight. Weight-bearing exercise is also important to help build bone density. Doctors recommend that everyone does at least 20 minutes of strenuous exercise, three times a week.

Sleep

Sleep is essential to your mental, physical, and emotional health, particularly when you are young and you are growing so quickly. As you sleep, the pituitary gland in your brain releases growth hormone, which helps build strong bone and muscle tissue. If you feel tired, it's your body's way of saying it needs some rest. Don't skimp on your beauty sleep!

Breath of fresh air

Getting out and about is an easy way to give your physical and mental health a kick start. Regular fresh air, sunlight, and exercise will help you to feel refreshed and vitalized. Don't just stay indoors in front of the TV or computer—go out and enjoy yourself!

The Human Genome

In 1986, scientists began an ambitious project to identify the human genome—the full set of genes that create a human being. The project is now complete. Scientists are using the information to track down the causes of inherited diseases. In the future, they may be able to treat these illnesses using gene therapy (see pages 10-11).

Drinking and smoking

Smoking and drinking damage your body's cells. Smoking causes some cancers and leads to respiratory diseases. Too much alcohol can damage the liver, kidneys, brain, nerves, and heart. Some people think that smoking and drinking are grown-up things to do, but they are at a huge cost to your health.

Eating well

A balanced diet is essential for healthy growth. Your diet should include a wide variety of foods. Fish, eggs, meat, and dairy products provide protein and also fats. Bread, potatoes, rice, and pasta yield carbohydrates. Fruits and vegetables are good sources of vitamins and minerals. Cereal, beans, and vegetables provide fiber for digestion. It's also vital to drink plenty of water.

Your body's changing needs

As cells divide, young human bodies get bigger and stronger, until adulthood. In later life, the body may lose a little height as disks between your backbones shrink, and your muscles weaken. At different stages of life, your body has different needs in terms of exercise, diet, and sleep. Stay fit and healthy by taking good care of your body and responding to its needs.

Amazing facts

Everyone grows at slightly different rates. Girls tend to grow faster than boys and stop earlier. You reach your full height in your late teens, but your bones and skeleton continue to change throughout your life.

Family sizes vary around the world. In some countries, children are seen as a source of valuable labor and support their parents in old age. Elsewhere, children are a sign of wealth and status. In most developed countries, family sizes are getting smaller.

The ovaries of a newborn baby girl contain all the eggs she will ever produce—about 500,000 eggs. By the time she is ready to menstruate, most of these have died off, but thousands remain. In contrast, a man produces around 1.8 trillion sperm during his lifetime.

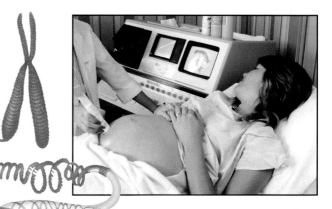

Most pregnancies last 40 weeks, but some last up to 43 weeks, some as few as 26 weeks.

There are between 100,000 and 200,000 genes needed to create a human body.

Glossary

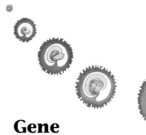

Cells The tiny units from which living things are made.

Cervix The narrow opening of the womb.

Chromosomes The tiny, x-shaped structures found in the nucleus of cells. They contain coded instructions for life and are made of molecules of DNA.

Clone An animal or plant that has developed from a single cell. A clone is identical to the plant or animal it was taken from.

Conception When a male's sperm fuses with a female's egg, to start a new life. Also called fertilization.

DNA (deoxyribonucleic acid). The "molecule of life," which contains instructions to build a new body, in coded sequences called genes.

Embryo A developing, unborn baby that is less than eight weeks old.

Fallopian tube One of the tubes that leads from the ovaries to the womb.

Fetus A developing, unborn baby that is more than eight weeks old.

Gene A section of DNA that carries a particular inherited characteristic, such as eye or hair color.

Genetic engineering A new technique that changes the features of a species.

Gestation The period between conception and birth.

Hormone A body chemical that regulates the working of a body part.

Molecule The smallest unit of a chemical compound that can exist.

Ovaries Two glands that produce female sex cells (eggs) as part of the female reproductive system.

Placenta A blood-rich organ that develops in the womb to nourish the unborn baby. It is expelled when the baby is born.

Testes Two glands that produce male sex cells (sperm) as part of the male reproductive system.

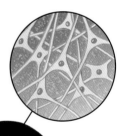

Index

Photo credits

Abbreviations: l-left, r-right, b-bottom, t-top, c-center, m-middle

All photos supplied by PBD except for: Front cover, 18ml, 26mr, 30bl – Digital Vision. 4tr – Photodisc. 6bl, 17t, 18br – Digital Stock. 6mr – Select Pictures. 7tl, 11mr, 16mr, 18bl, 19mr, 27ml, 27br, 28bl, 30mr – Corbis. 8br – Quest/Science Photo Library. 11tl all, 19b all, 20bl, 20bml, 20bmr, 21ml, 30tr – Roger Vlitos. 11br, 29trt, 29trb, 29mrt, 29mrc, 29mrb – Stockbyte. 15bl – Ken Hammond/USDA. 19ml – Nick Oakes/Science Photo Library. 20ml, 21bl, 23mr – Brand X Pictures. 21tr all, 25bl, 27mr, 29trc – Corel. 21br – John Paul Kay/Peter Arnold Inc./Science Photo Library. 25br, 28br – Image 100. 27t – Flat Earth.Lovegrove/ Science Photo Library. 30bl – Corbis Royalty Free.